Refuse to Use

Cynthia MacGregor

READING ROOM

New York

Published in 2003 by The Rosen Publishing Group, Inc.
29 East 21st Street, New York, NY 10010

Copyright © 2003 by The Rosen Publishing Group, Inc.

First Library Edition 2003

All rights reserved. No part of this book may be reproduced in any form without permission in writing from the publisher, except by a reviewer.

Book Design: Ron A. Churley

Photo Credits: Cover, p. 1 © SW Productions/Index Stock; p. 4 © Noble Stock/ International Stock; pp. 6, 12, 14–15 © Michael Krasowitz/FPG International; p. 7 © Telegraph Colour Library/FPG International; p. 8 © Barbara Peacock/FPG International; p. 11 © Denis Boissavy/FPG International; p. 17 by Ron A. Churley; p. 18 © William Adams/FPG International; p. 19 © Kevin Cruff/FPG International; p. 20 © Fredde Lieberman/Index Stock; p. 21 © C. Gatewood/ The Image Works; p. 22 © J. Taposchaner/FPG International.

Library of Congress Cataloging-in-Publication Data

MacGregor, Cynthia.
  Refuse to use / Cynthia MacGregor.
    p. cm. — (The Rosen Publishing Group's reading room collection)
Summary: Discusses drugs and the dangers of using them.
  ISBN 978-1-4358-8992-7
  1. Drug abuse—Juvenile literature. 2. Drugs of abuse—Juvenile literature. [1. Drug abuse. 2. Drugs of abuse.] I. Title. II. Series.
  HV5809.5 .M33 2002
  362.29—dc21
                    2001007480

Manufactured in the United States of America

For More Information
The National Clearinghouse for Alcohol and Drug Information: For Kids Only
http://www.health.org/kidsarea/index.htm

Contents

Taking Bad Chances	5
"Everybody's Doing It"	6
What Alcohol Does	9
A Sick Feeling	10
Tobacco and Your Body	13
How Tobacco Controls You	14
Good Drugs, Bad Drugs	16
Drugs and Your Heart	18
Drugs and Your Brain	20
Refuse to Use!	22
Glossary	23
Index	24

Taking Bad Chances

Some young people do **dangerous** things, like crossing the street without looking or playing with matches. Another dangerous thing a young person can do is use drugs, **alcohol**, or **tobacco**.

Drugs are **chemicals** that change how you think, feel, and act. Alcohol is a drug in some kinds of drinks, like beer and wine. Tobacco is a plant that some people smoke or chew. Alcohol, tobacco, and other drugs can do bad things to your body.

> You can choose to stay healthy by not using drugs, alcohol, and tobacco.

"Everybody's Doing It"

Some young people think using drugs, alcohol, and tobacco seems like a grown-up thing to do. Some wonder what it feels like to smoke a cigarette, use chewing tobacco, drink a beer, or take drugs.

It's best to stay away from drugs, alcohol, and tobacco, even if it seems like most of your friends are trying them.

Some people think it's "cool" to smoke. You can choose to be healthy instead and say no.

Some young people use drugs, alcohol, and tobacco because their friends use them. Their friends may say, "We're doing it. Why don't you?" A real friend wouldn't ask you to hurt yourself by using these things.

What Alcohol Does

Alcohol affects your brain. Your brain controls everything you do. It controls how you walk, talk, think, and breathe.

When a person drinks alcohol, his brain slows down and doesn't work like it should. Simple things like walking and talking can be hard to do. The person acts differently and may do things he usually wouldn't. If he tries to drive a car, he might crash it. He might hurt himself or hurt others.

> If you drink too much alcohol, you may stop caring about things that are important.

A Sick Feeling

Drinking alcohol can make a person sick. When a person drinks alcohol, his body can't work right. If he drinks too much, it can make him so sick that he throws up. He might have to lie in bed all day because his head hurts.

When a person drinks alcohol regularly, he can become **addicted** to it. He might think he needs to drink alcohol to deal with life. A person who is addicted to alcohol is called an **alcoholic**.

Alcoholics may forget things they said and did while they were drinking.

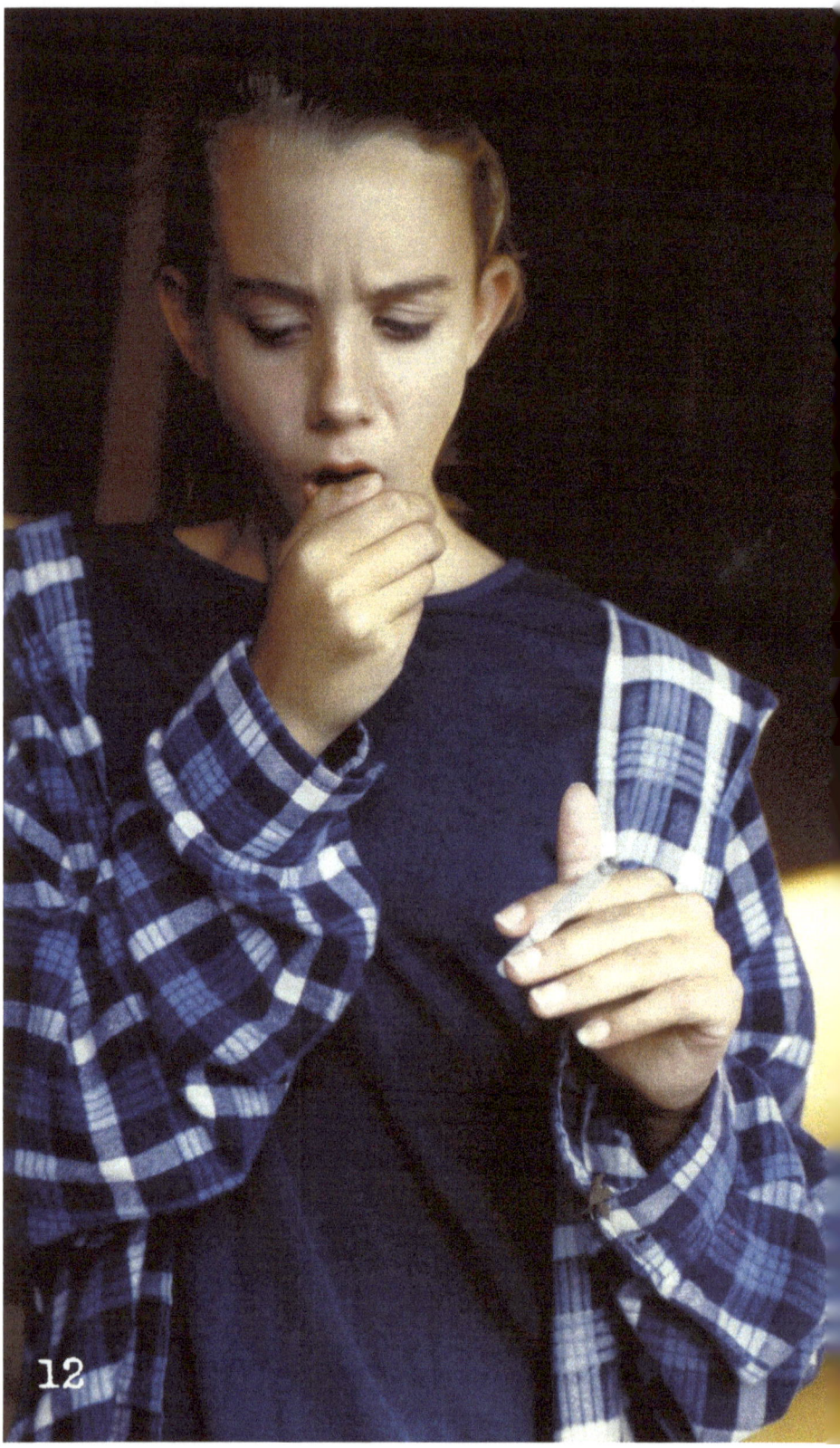

Tobacco and Your Body

Cigarettes and chewing tobacco are made from the tobacco plant. When a person smokes a cigarette, she breathes in **tar**. The tar coats her lungs and makes it hard for her to breathe. She may cough (KOFF) a lot. When a person chews tobacco, it harms her teeth and gums. She may even have to have part of her jaw removed.

Cigarettes and chewing tobacco have thousands of poisons in them. Some of these poisons cause cancer. Cancer is a sickness that can kill people.

About forty-five people in the United States die every hour from smoking.

How Tobacco Controls You

Cigarettes and chewing tobacco have something in them called **nicotine**. Nicotine is addictive. This means that once a person's body gets used to it, it needs more. Nicotine is also poisonous. Just one thimbleful could kill an adult.

Nicotine makes the heart beat faster and might make the smoker feel nervous. After years of smoking, nicotine can hurt the smoker's heart.

Many people start smoking without knowing how hard it is to quit.

Good Drugs, Bad Drugs

Some drugs, like medicines, can help you. Your doctor or your parent may give you medicine to make you feel better when you are sick. It is important to always ask your parents about any medicine before you take it.

Some drugs can hurt you. Many of these drugs are illegal. It is against the law to buy, use, or sell them. These drugs can hurt your mind and your body.

> Your parent can make sure you take the right amount of medicine to make you well. Taking too much medicine can be dangerous.

Drugs and Your Heart

Stimulants (STIM-you-lents) are drugs that make the heart beat faster. If a person's heart beats too fast, it can kill them.

Cocaine, a powder that is sniffed, is a stimulant. "Crack," a solid form of cocaine that is smoked, is also a stimulant.

Some drugs can kill you by making your heart beat too fast.

Depressants (dih-PRESS-ents) are drugs that slow the body down. Alcohol and pills called **barbiturates** (bar-BIH-chur-its) are depressants. They can slow a person's body down so much that he or she dies.

Barbiturates slow a person's heart down and can cause death.

Drugs and Your Brain

Some drugs make people see and think things that aren't real. Drugs like **marijuana** (mair-ih-WAH-nah) and LSD affect how the brain works. People who use these drugs may take risks because they think they can't get hurt. Someone who smokes marijuana may forget things and flunk out of school.

Some people call marijuana "grass," "pot," "weed," or "dope."

Heroin (HAIR-oh-in), which is usually shot into the veins, can make a person stop caring whether she eats or sleeps. A person on heroin may care only about getting more heroin.

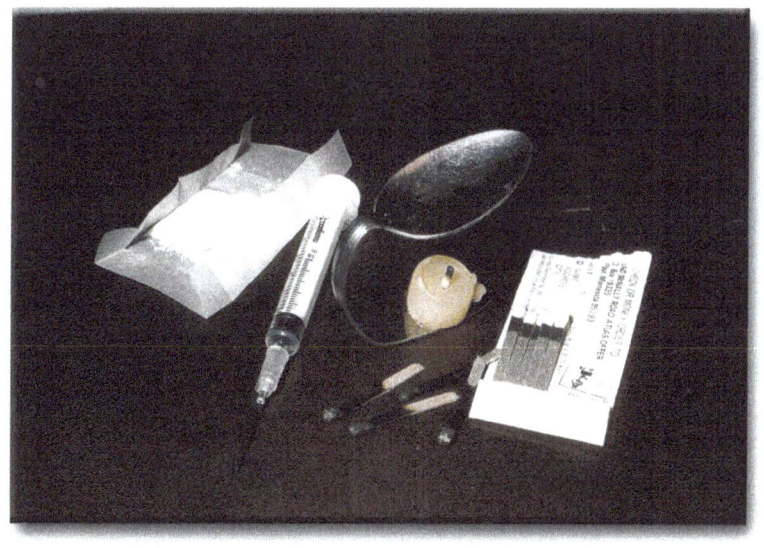

Heroin is sometimes called "smack" or "china white."

Refuse to Use!

Something that seems harmless, like glue, is sometimes used as a drug. Glue is an **inhalant**. Inhalants are household products that make you feel weird when you breathe them in. Inhalants can harm your brain, lungs, and heart. They can even kill you!

Be smart and grown-up—refuse to use. If someone offers you a cigarette, alcohol, or a pill, say no. If someone offers you marijuana, an inhalant, or any drug at all, say no. Saying no doesn't make you uncool. Saying no makes you smart!

Glossary

addicted When someone needs a drug to deal with everyday life.

alcohol Something people drink that can cause them to become drunk.

alcoholic Someone who is addicted to alcohol.

barbiturate A drug taken in pill form that slows down your body.

chemical Something that changes the way you think, feel, or act.

cocaine An addictive drug in powder form that is sniffed through the nose.

dangerous Not safe. Harmful.

heroin An addictive drug that is usually shot into a person's veins.

inhalant A household product that some people use as a drug by breathing in its fumes.

marijuana A drug people smoke that is made from the leaves of a plant.

nicotine A poisonous, addictive chemical found in tobacco.

tar A poisonous, brownish-black element from cigarette smoke.

tobacco A plant whose leaves are dried, cut up, and smoked. Cigarettes have tobacco in them.

Index

A
addicted(ive), 10, 14
alcohol(ic), 5, 6, 7, 9, 10, 18, 22

B
barbiturates, 18
beer, 5, 6
brain, 9, 20, 22

C
cancer, 13
cigarette(s), 6, 13, 14, 22
cocaine, 18
"crack," 18

D
depressants, 18, 19

G
glue, 22

H
heart, 14, 18, 22
heroin, 21

I
inhalant(s), 22

L
LSD, 20
lungs, 13, 22

M
marijuana, 20, 22

N
nicotine, 14

S
stimulant(s), 18

T
tar, 13
tobacco, 5, 6, 7, 13, 14

W
wine, 5

www.ingramcontent.com/pod-product-compliance
Lightning Source LLC
Chambersburg PA
CBHW041220070526
44584CB00001B/31